es • best-loved cookies • best-loved

cookies • best-loved cookies • best-

-loved cookies • best-loved cookies

es • best-loved cookies • best-loved

cookies • best-loved cookies • best-

-loved cookies • best-loved cookies

es • best-loved cookies • best-loved

cookies • best-loved cookies • best-

-loved cookies • best-loved cookies

es • best-loved cookies • best-loved

cookies • best-loved cookies • best-

-loved cookies • best-loved cookies

best-loved
cookies

How the Legendary
Toll House Cookie Came to Be

The Toll House Cookie got its name from a lovely old tollhouse located between Boston and New Bedford, Massachusetts. Built in 1709, the house had long been a haven for weary travelers in search of food, drink and a change of horses.

The historic old house was purchased by Mr. and Mrs. Wakefield in 1930 and turned into the now-famous Toll House Inn. In keeping with tradition, Mrs. Wakefield baked for her guests, perfecting and improving upon many old recipes. Soon, her tasty desserts attracted people from all over New England.

One day, while stirring together a batch of Butter Drop Do cookies, a favorite Colonial recipe, Mrs. Wakefield cut a bar of Nestlé Semi-Sweet Chocolate into bits and added them to her cookie dough, expecting them to melt. Instead, the chocolate held its shape, softening to a creamy texture. This delicious discovery was dubbed the Toll House Cookie, which became a widespread favorite. With Mrs. Wakefield's permission, we put the recipe on the wrapper of our Nestlé Semi-Sweet Chocolate Bar.

As the popularity of the Toll House Cookie continued to grow, we looked for ways to make this cookie easier to bake. First, we produced a special, scored chocolate bar that could be divided into small sections. Then we began offering tiny pieces of chocolate in convenient packages—and that's how the first Real Nestlé® Toll House® Semi-Sweet Chocolate Morsels were introduced.

Since they were first created for the Toll House Cookie, Nestlé Semi-Sweet Morsels have satisfied the chocolate cravings of millions. Today, they're used to make hundreds of delectable chocolate goodies all across America.

Nestlé is pleased to present our chocolate-lovers' cookie collection on the following pages. With over 70 recipes, you'll find all your favorite cookies and bars, plus many new ones, straight from the Toll House Kitchen to yours.

Best-Loved Cookies

Pictured on Cover: Original Nestlé Toll House Chocolate Chip Cookies, Double Chocolate Dream Cookies, Macadamia Nut White Chip Pumpkin Cookies, Choc-Oat-Chip Cookies, White Chip Orange Cookies and Oatmeal Scotchies (see index for recipe page numbers)

© *Copyright 1995 Nestlé. All rights reserved.*
Produced by Meredith Custom Publishing, 1912 Grand Ave., Des Moines, Iowa 50309-3379.
Canadian GST Reg. #R123482887. Printed in the U.S.A.

Chocolat

Ever since Mrs. Wakefield used Nestlé chocolate to invent the Original Toll House Cookie, the Nestlé name has been synonymous with home-baked goodness. Inspiring delighted smiles and warm childhood memories of sweet aromas drifting from the oven, the recipes in this chapter have become the most requested and enjoyed, earning them a proud place in our Chocolate Hall of Fame.

Chocolate Turtle Brownies
(see recipe, page 8),
Frosted Double Chocolate
Cookies (see recipe, page 9)
and Original Nestlé Toll House
Chocolate Chip Cookies
(Bar Cookie Variation)
(see recipe, page 6)

Hall of Fame

Original Nestlé Toll House
Chocolate Chip Cookies

2¼ cups all-purpose flour
1 teaspoon baking soda
1 teaspoon salt
1 cup butter or margarine, softened
¾ cup granulated sugar
¾ cup packed brown sugar

1 teaspoon vanilla extract
2 eggs
2 cups (12-ounce package) NESTLÉ TOLL HOUSE Semi-Sweet Chocolate Morsels
1 cup chopped DIAMOND Walnuts

Combine flour, baking soda and salt in small bowl. Beat butter, granulated sugar, brown sugar and vanilla in large mixer bowl until creamy. Add eggs one at a time, beating well after each addition. Gradually beat in flour mixture. Stir in morsels and walnuts. Drop by rounded tablespoon onto ungreased baking sheets.

Bake in preheated 375°F. oven for 9 to 11 minutes or until golden brown. Let stand for 2 minutes; remove to wire racks to cool completely. Makes about 5 dozen cookies.

Bar Cookie Variation: Prepare dough as *above*. Spread into greased 15 x 10-inch jelly-roll pan. Bake in preheated 375°F. oven for 20 to 25 minutes or until golden brown. Cool completely in pan on wire rack. Cut into bars. Makes 4 dozen.

Pictured on pages 4 and 5.

Slice-and-Bake Cookie Variation: Prepare dough as *above*. Divide in half; wrap each half in waxed paper. Chill for 1 hour or until firm. Shape each half into 15-inch log; wrap in waxed paper. Chill for 30 minutes.* Cut into ½-inch-thick slices; place on ungreased baking sheets. Bake in preheated 375°F. oven for 8 to 10 minutes or until golden brown. Let stand for 2 minutes; remove to wire racks to cool completely. Makes about 5 dozen cookies.

*Note: Logs may be stored in refrigerator for up to 1 week or in freezer for up to 8 weeks.

Original Nestlé Toll House
Chocolate Chip Cookies

Chocolate Turtle Brownies

2 cups (12-ounce package) NESTLÉ TOLL HOUSE
  Semi-Sweet Chocolate Morsels, *divided*
½ cup (1 stick) butter or margarine, cut into pieces
3 eggs
1¼ cups all-purpose flour
1 cup granulated sugar

1 teaspoon vanilla extract
¼ teaspoon baking soda
½ cup chopped DIAMOND Walnuts
12 caramels
1 tablespoon milk

Melt *1 cup* morsels and butter in large, *heavy* saucepan over *lowest possible* heat, stirring constantly until smooth. Remove from heat; stir in eggs. Add flour, granulated sugar, vanilla and baking soda; stir well. Spread batter into greased 13 x 9-inch baking pan; sprinkle with *remaining* morsels and walnuts.

Bake in preheated 350°F. oven for 20 to 25 minutes or until wooden pick inserted in center comes out slightly sticky.

Microwave caramels and milk in small, microwave-safe bowl on HIGH (100%) power for 1 minute; stir. Microwave at additional 10- to 20-second intervals, stirring until smooth. Drizzle over warm brownies. Cool completely in pan on wire rack. Cut into bars.
Makes 2 dozen brownies.

Pictured on pages 4 and 5.

Masterful Melting

The key to melting chocolate successfully is to use slow and gentle heat.

To melt NESTLÉ TOLL HOUSE Semi-Sweet Chocolate Morsels, Mint Morsels or broken-up Semi-Sweet or Unsweetened Chocolate Baking Bars, microwave 1 cup (6 ounces) in an uncovered microwave-safe bowl on HIGH (100%) power for 1 minute; stir. Microwave at additional 10- to 20-second intervals, stirring after each interval, until chocolate is smooth.

For the more delicate products—Milk Chocolate Morsels, Butterscotch Flavored Morsels, Premier White Morsels or Premier White Baking Bars— melt as above except use 70% power.

Or, melt morsels or baking bars in a heavy-gauge saucepan on lowest possible heat. When chocolate begins to melt and become shiny, remove from heat; stir. Return to heat for a few seconds at a time, stirring until smooth. (This method is not recommended for the more delicate morsels and baking bars.)

Frosted Double Chocolate Cookies

2 cups (12-ounce package) NESTLÉ TOLL HOUSE
Semi-Sweet Chocolate Morsels, *divided*

1¼ cups all-purpose flour

¾ teaspoon baking soda

½ teaspoon salt

½ cup (1 stick) butter or margarine, softened

½ cup packed brown sugar

¼ cup granulated sugar

1 teaspoon vanilla extract

1 egg

½ cup chopped nuts (optional)

Chocolate Frosting (recipe follows)

Microwave ¾ *cup* morsels in small, microwave-safe bowl on HIGH (100%) power for 1 minute; stir. Microwave at additional 10- to 20-second intervals, stirring until smooth; cool to room temperature.

Combine flour, baking soda and salt in small bowl. Beat butter, brown sugar, granulated sugar and vanilla in large mixer bowl until creamy. Beat in melted chocolate and egg. Gradually beat in flour mixture. Stir in ¾ *cup* morsels and nuts. Drop by rounded tablespoon onto ungreased baking sheets.

Bake in preheated 375°F. oven for 8 to 9 minutes or until edges are set but centers are still slightly soft. Let stand for 3 minutes; remove to wire racks to cool completely. Spread Chocolate Frosting on cookies. Makes about 2½ dozen cookies.

For Chocolate Frosting: Microwave *remaining* ½ *cup* morsels and 2 tablespoons butter or margarine in medium, microwave-safe bowl on HIGH (100%) power for 30 seconds; stir. Microwave at additional 10- to 20-second intervals, stirring until smooth. Add 1¼ cups sifted powdered sugar and 2 tablespoons milk; stir until smooth.

Pictured on pages 4 and 5.

Oatmeal Scotchies

1¼ cups all-purpose flour
1 teaspoon baking soda
½ teaspoon salt
½ teaspoon ground cinnamon
1 cup (2 sticks) LAND O LAKES Butter, softened
¾ cup granulated sugar

¾ cup packed brown sugar
2 eggs
1 teaspoon vanilla extract or grated orange peel
3 cups quick or old-fashioned oats
1⅔ cups (11-ounce package) NESTLÉ TOLL HOUSE Butterscotch Flavored Morsels

Combine flour, baking soda, salt and cinnamon in small bowl. Beat butter, granulated sugar, brown sugar, eggs and vanilla in large mixer bowl until creamy. Gradually beat in flour mixture. Stir in oats and morsels. Drop by rounded tablespoon onto ungreased baking sheets.

Bake in preheated 375°F. oven for 7 to 8 minutes for chewy cookies or 9 to 10 minutes for crispy cookies. Let stand for 2 minutes; remove to wire racks to cool completely. Makes about 4 dozen cookies.

Bar Cookie Variation: Prepare dough as *above*. Spread dough into greased 15 x 10-inch jelly-roll pan. Bake in preheated 375°F. oven for 18 to 22 minutes or until very lightly browned. Cool completely in pan on rack.
Makes 4 dozen.

Cookies on Call

Be prepared for special occasions, last-minute gatherings or snacktime anytime by keeping cookies or dough on hand in the freezer. Place cookie dough in freezer bags or storage containers and freeze for up to two months. Thaw the dough, sealed, at room temperature, and bake as usual.

Freeze baked cookies, that have been cooled, for up to three or four months. For snacks, wrap two cookies, back to back in freezer wrap. Or, freeze cookies in freezer bags or storage containers. Thaw cookies, sealed, at room temperature. For a fresh-baked taste, place thawed cookies on baking sheets. Bake in a preheated 300°F. oven for a few minutes or until heated through. Serve immediately.

Oatmeal Scotchies

Blonde Brownies

2¼ cups all-purpose flour
2½ teaspoons baking powder
½ teaspoon salt
1¾ cups packed brown sugar
¾ cup (1½ sticks) butter or margarine, softened

1 teaspoon vanilla extract
3 eggs
2 cups (12-ounce package) NESTLÉ TOLL HOUSE Semi-Sweet Chocolate Morsels

Combine flour, baking powder and salt in small bowl. Beat brown sugar, butter and vanilla in large mixer bowl until creamy. Add eggs, one at a time, beating well after each addition. Gradually beat in flour mixture. Stir in morsels. Spread into greased 15 x 10-inch jelly-roll pan.

Bake in preheated 350°F. oven for 20 to 25 minutes or until top is golden brown. Cool completely in pan on wire rack. Cut into bars. Makes 35 brownies.

Left to right: White Chip Chocolate Cookies (see recipe opposite page), Blonde Brownies (see recipe above) and Mini Morsel Meringue Cookies (see recipe, page 14)

White Chip Chocolate Cookies

2¼ cups all-purpose flour

⅔ cup NESTLÉ TOLL HOUSE Baking Cocoa

1 teaspoon baking soda

¼ teaspoon salt

1 cup (2 sticks) butter or margarine, softened

¾ cup granulated sugar

⅔ cup packed brown sugar

1 teaspoon vanilla extract

2 eggs

2 cups (12-ounce package) NESTLÉ TOLL HOUSE Premier White Morsels

Combine flour, cocoa, baking soda and salt in small bowl. Beat butter, granulated sugar, brown sugar and vanilla in large mixer bowl until creamy. Beat in eggs, one at a time, beating well after each addition. Gradually beat in flour mixture. Stir in morsels. Drop by well-rounded teaspoon onto ungreased baking sheets.

Bake in preheated 350°F. oven for 9 to 11 minutes or until centers are set. Let stand for 2 minutes; remove to wire racks to cool completely. Makes about 5 dozen cookies.

Mini Morsel Meringue Cookies

4 egg whites
½ teaspoon salt
½ teaspoon cream of tartar

1 cup granulated sugar
2 cups (12-ounce package) NESTLÉ TOLL HOUSE Semi-Sweet Chocolate Mini Morsels

Beat egg whites, salt and cream of tartar in small mixer bowl until soft peaks form. Gradually beat in granulated sugar until stiff peaks form (see photo, *below*). Gently fold in morsels, ⅓ at a time. Drop by level tablespoon onto greased baking sheets.

Bake in preheated 300°F. oven for 20 to 25 minutes or until cookies are dry and crisp.

Let stand for 2 minutes; remove to wire racks to cool completely. Store in airtight containers. Makes about 5 dozen cookies.

Pictured on pages 12 and 13.

For stiff peaks, continue beating the egg-white mixture, gradually adding the sugar, until the mixture looks glossy and the peaks stand straight when the beaters are lifted.

Choc-Oat-Chip Cookies

1¾ cups all-purpose flour

1 teaspoon baking soda

½ teaspoon salt (optional)

1¼ cups packed light brown sugar

1 cup (2 sticks) LAND O LAKES Butter, softened

½ cup granulated sugar

2 eggs

2 tablespoons milk

2 teaspoons vanilla extract

2½ cups quick or old-fashioned oats

2 cups (12-ounce package) NESTLÉ TOLL HOUSE Semi-Sweet Chocolate Morsels

1 cup coarsely chopped nuts (optional)

Combine flour, baking soda and salt in small bowl. Beat brown sugar, butter and granulated sugar in large mixer bowl until creamy. Beat in eggs, milk and vanilla. Gradually beat in flour mixture. Stir in oats, morsels and nuts. Drop by rounded tablespoon onto ungreased baking sheets.

Better Baking with Butter and Margarine

For baking, the Toll House Test Kitchen suggests using butter or regular stick margarine for best results. However, if you prefer using a lower-fat margarine, choose one with no less than 60% vegetable oil. Products labeled as "spread" and "diet" contain less fat and more water. They tend to produce a cookie that is more cake-like and less crisp around the edges.

Bake in preheated 375°F. oven for 9 to 10 minutes for chewy cookies or 12 to 13 minutes for crispy cookies. Let stand for 1 minute; remove to wire racks to cool completely. Makes about 4 dozen cookies.

Pictured on page 17.

Chunky Chocolate Chip Peanut Butter Cookies

1¼ cups all-purpose flour
½ teaspoon baking soda
½ teaspoon salt
½ teaspoon ground cinnamon
¾ cup (1½ sticks) butter or margarine, softened
½ cup granulated sugar
½ cup packed brown sugar

½ cup creamy peanut butter
1 egg
1 teaspoon vanilla extract
2 cups (12-ounce package) NESTLÉ TOLL HOUSE Semi-Sweet Chocolate Morsels
½ cup coarsely chopped peanuts

Combine flour, baking soda, salt and cinnamon in small bowl. Beat butter, granulated sugar, brown sugar and peanut butter in large mixer bowl until creamy. Beat in egg and vanilla. Gradually beat in flour mixture. Stir in morsels and peanuts. Drop dough by rounded tablespoon onto ungreased baking sheets. Press down slightly to flatten into 2-inch circles.

Bake in preheated 375°F. oven for 7 to 10 minutes or until edges are set but centers are still soft. Let stand for 4 minutes; remove to wire racks to cool completely. Makes about 3 dozen cookies.

Cookie Care-Packages

When you plan to mail cookies, choose a recipe for firm cookies, avoiding soft, brittle or delicate varieties. Cookies tend to taste fresher longer when made with regular stick margarine instead of butter. After baking, cool completely, then wrap two cookies at a time, back to back in plastic wrap. Stack cookies snugly, on end, in a sturdy box, using a filler such as bubble wrap, foam packing pieces or crumpled waxed paper or paper towels to fill in extra spaces. Seal, label and mail.

Chunky Chocolate Chip Peanut Butter Cookies (see recipe above) and Choc-Oat-Chip Cookies (see recipe, page 15)

Chocolate Butterscotch Cereal Bars

1 cup granulated sugar

1 cup light corn syrup

1 cup creamy peanut butter

6 cups crisp rice cereal

1 cup (6 ounces) NESTLÉ TOLL HOUSE Semi-Sweet Chocolate Morsels

1 cup (6 ounces) NESTLÉ TOLL HOUSE Butterscotch Flavored Morsels

Combine granulated sugar and corn syrup in large saucepan; bring *just to a boil* over medium heat, stirring constantly. Remove from heat; stir in peanut butter. Stir in cereal. Press into greased 13 x 9-inch baking pan.

Microwave chocolate and butterscotch morsels in medium, microwave-safe bowl on HIGH (100%) power for 1 minute; stir. Microwave at additional 10- to 20-second intervals, stirring until smooth. Spread over cereal mixture. Chill in pan for 20 minutes or until firm. Cut into bars. Makes 4 dozen bars.

Chocolate Butterscotch Cereal Bars

Like gift-giving and family gatherings, baking and sharing cookies is a holiday tradition, with treasured recipes passed from friend to friend and handed down through generations. Add to your family's collection of special-occasion cookies with such festive treats as Chocolate Raspberry Layer Bars, Swirl-of-Chocolate Cheesecake Triangles and Chocolate Cherry Thumbprints.

Chocolate Cherry Thumbprints

2 cups (12-ounce package) NESTLÉ TOLL HOUSE Semi-Sweet Chocolate Morsels, *divided*

1¾ cups quick or old-fashioned oats

1½ cups all-purpose flour

¼ cup NESTLÉ TOLL HOUSE Baking Cocoa

1 teaspoon baking powder

¼ teaspoon salt (optional)

¾ cup granulated sugar

⅔ cup butter or margarine, softened

2 eggs

1 teaspoon vanilla extract

2 cups (two 10-ounce jars) maraschino cherries, drained and patted dry

Microwave *1 cup* morsels in small, microwave-safe bowl on HIGH (100%) power for 1 minute; stir. Microwave at additional 10- to 20-second intervals, stirring until smooth. Cool to room temperature. Combine oats, flour, cocoa, baking powder and salt in medium bowl. Beat granulated sugar, butter, eggs and vanilla in large mixer bowl until smooth. Beat in melted chocolate. Stir in oat mixture. Cover; chill dough for 1 hour. Shape dough into 1-inch balls. Place 2 inches apart on ungreased baking sheet. Press deep centers with thumb. Place maraschino cherry into each center.

Bake in preheated 350°F. oven 10 to 12 minutes or until set. Let stand 2 minutes; remove to wire racks to cool completely. Melt *remaining* morsels as above; drizzle over cookies. Makes 4 dozen.

n Cookies

Chocolate Cherry Thumbprints (see recipe opposite), Chocolate Raspberry Layer Bars (see recipe, page 22), Chocolate Mini Chip Holiday Cookies (see recipe, page 23) and Swirl-of-Chocolate Cheesecake Triangles (see recipe, page 27)

Chocolate Raspberry Layer Bars

1⅔ cups graham cracker crumbs

½ cup (1 stick) butter or margarine, melted

2 cups (12-ounce package) NESTLÉ TOLL HOUSE Semi-Sweet Chocolate Morsels, *divided*

2⅔ cups (7-ounce package) flaked coconut

1¼ cups (14-ounce can) CARNATION® Sweetened Condensed Milk

1 cup seedless red raspberry jam

⅓ cup finely chopped DIAMOND Walnuts (optional)

⅓ cup NESTLÉ TOLL HOUSE Premier White Morsels

Combine graham cracker crumbs and butter in medium bowl. Press firmly onto bottom of ungreased 13 x 9-inch baking pan. Sprinkle with *1½ cups* semi-sweet morsels, then coconut; pour sweetened condensed milk evenly over top.

Bake in preheated 350°F. oven for 20 to 25 minutes or until lightly browned; cool completely in pan on wire rack.

Spread jam over cooled top; sprinkle with walnuts. Place *remaining* semi-sweet morsels and white morsels in separate heavy-duty plastic bags. Microwave together on MEDIUM-HIGH (70%) power for 45 seconds; knead bags to mix. Microwave at additional 10-second intervals, kneading until smooth. Cut a small hole in corner of each bag; squeeze to pipe over bars. Chill for 5 minutes to set chocolate. Cut into bars. Makes 2 dozen bars.

Pictured on pages 20 and 21.

Cookie Art

To add a playful touch to rolled cookies such as the Chocolate Mini Chip Holiday Cookies, *opposite page*, use any cookie cutters you like. Or, make a stencil by cutting your own pattern out of heavy paper. Use a knife to cut around the stencil onto rolled-out cookie dough.

Once the cookies are baked and cooled, decorate them with white frosting, either purchased or homemade. Tint the frosting with liquid food coloring for pastel shades or, for more vibrant colors, use paste coloring (available in specialty stores near cake-decorating supplies). For a thinner, glaze-like topping, stir a small amount of light corn syrup into prepared frosting. Add your choice of candies or colored sugars as a finishing touch.

Chocolate Mini Chip Holiday Cookies

1 cup (2 sticks) butter or margarine, softened
½ cup packed brown sugar
⅓ cup granulated sugar
2 teaspoons vanilla extract
½ teaspoon salt
1 egg yolk

2½ cups all-purpose flour
2 cups (12-ounce package) NESTLÉ TOLL HOUSE Semi-Sweet Chocolate Mini Morsels, *divided*
1 container (16 ounces) prepared vanilla frosting, colored if desired
Chocolate Drizzle (optional recipe follows)

Beat butter, brown sugar, granulated sugar, vanilla and salt in large mixer bowl until creamy. Beat in egg yolk. Gradually beat in flour. Stir in *1½ cups* morsels. Divide dough in half. Cover; chill for 1 hour or until firm.

Roll ½ of dough to ¼-inch thickness between 2 sheets of waxed paper. Remove top sheet of waxed paper. Cut dough into shapes (see Cookie Art tip box, *opposite page*). Lift from waxed paper; place on ungreased baking sheets. Chill for 10 minutes. Repeat with remaining dough.

Bake in preheated 350°F. oven for 9 to 11 minutes or until golden brown. Let stand for 2 minutes; remove to wire racks to cool completely. Spread or pipe with frosting as desired (see tip box, *opposite page*). Decorate with Chocolate Drizzle, if desired. Makes about 3 dozen cookies.

For Chocolate Drizzle: Place *remaining* morsels in heavy-duty plastic bag. Microwave on HIGH (100%) power for 45 seconds; knead bag to mix. Microwave at additional 10-second intervals, kneading until smooth. Cut a small hole in corner of bag; squeeze to pipe chocolate over frosted cookies.

Pictured on pages 20 and 21.

Chocolate Almond Biscotti

2 cups (12-ounce package) NESTLÉ TOLL HOUSE Semi-Sweet Chocolate Morsels, *divided*

2 cups all-purpose flour

¼ cup NESTLÉ TOLL HOUSE Baking Cocoa

1½ teaspoons baking powder

¼ teaspoon baking soda

¼ teaspoon salt

½ cup granulated sugar

½ cup packed brown sugar

¼ cup (½ stick) butter or margarine, softened

½ teaspoon vanilla extract

½ teaspoon almond extract

3 eggs

1 cup slivered almonds, toasted

Chocolate Coating (optional recipe follows)

Microwave *1 cup* morsels in small, microwave-safe bowl on HIGH (100%) power 1 minute; stir. Microwave at additional 10- to 20-second intervals, stirring until smooth. Cool to room temperature.

Combine flour, cocoa, baking powder, baking soda and salt in medium bowl. Beat granulated sugar, brown sugar, butter, vanilla and almond extract in mixer bowl until crumbly. Add eggs, one at a time, beating well after each. Beat in melted chocolate. Gradually beat in flour mixture. Stir in almonds. Chill for 15 minutes or until firm. Shape dough with floured hands into 2 loaves (3 inches wide by 1 inch high) on 1 large or 2 small greased baking sheet(s).

Bake in preheated 325°F. oven for 40 to 50 minutes or until firm. Let stand 15 minutes. Cut into ¾-inch-thick slices; turn slices on their sides. Bake for 10 minutes on *each* side or until dry. Remove to wire racks to cool completely. If desired, dip each biscotti halfway into Chocolate Coating, pushing mixture up onto cookie with a spatula; shake off excess. Place on waxed-paper-lined baking sheets. Chill for 10 minutes or until chocolate is set. Store in airtight containers in cool place or chill. Makes 2½ dozen biscotti.

For Chocolate Coating: Microwave *remaining* morsels and 2 tablespoons shortening in microwave-safe bowl on HIGH (100%) power for 1 minute; stir. Microwave at additional 10- to 20-second intervals, stirring until smooth.

Chocolate Almond Biscotti (see recipe above) and
Chocolate-Dipped Brandy Snaps (see recipe, page 26)

Chocolate-Dipped Brandy Snaps

½ cup (1 stick) butter
½ cup granulated sugar
⅓ cup dark corn syrup
½ teaspoon ground cinnamon
¼ teaspoon ground ginger
1 cup all-purpose flour

2 teaspoons brandy
1 cup (6 ounces) NESTLÉ TOLL HOUSE
  Semi-Sweet Chocolate Morsels
1 tablespoon shortening
⅓ cup chopped nuts

Melt butter, granulated sugar, corn syrup, cinnamon and ginger in medium saucepan over low heat, stirring until smooth. Remove from heat; stir in flour and brandy. Drop by rounded teaspoon about 3 inches apart onto ungreased baking sheets, baking no more than 6 at a time.

Bake in preheated 300°F. oven for 10 to 14 minutes or until deep caramel color. Let stand for a few seconds. Remove from baking sheets and immediately roll around wooden spoon handle; cool.

Microwave morsels and shortening in small, microwave-safe bowl on HIGH (100%) power for 45 seconds; stir. Microwave at additional 10- to 20-second intervals, stirring until smooth.

Dip each cookie halfway into melted chocolate mixture, pushing mixture up onto cookie with a spatula; shake off excess. Sprinkle with nuts; place on waxed-paper-lined baking sheets. Chill for 10 minutes or until chocolate is set. Store in airtight containers in refrigerator. Makes about 3 dozen cookies.

Pictured on page 25.

Swirl-of-Chocolate Cheesecake Triangles

CRUST
- 2 cups graham cracker crumbs
- ½ cup (1 stick) butter or margarine, melted
- ⅓ cup granulated sugar

FILLING
- 2 packages (8 ounces *each*) cream cheese, softened
- 1 cup granulated sugar
- ¼ cup all-purpose flour
- 1½ cups (12-fluid-ounce can) CARNATION Evaporated Milk
- 2 eggs
- 1 tablespoon vanilla extract
- 1 cup (6 ounces) NESTLÉ TOLL HOUSE Semi-Sweet Chocolate Morsels

For Crust: Combine crumbs, butter and granulated sugar in medium bowl; press onto bottom of ungreased 13 x 9-inch baking pan.

For Filling: Beat cream cheese, granulated sugar and flour in large mixer bowl until smooth. Gradually beat in evaporated milk, eggs and vanilla.

Microwave morsels in medium, microwave-safe bowl on HIGH (100%) power for 1 minute; stir. Microwave at additional 10- to 20-second intervals, stirring until smooth.

Stir *1 cup* cream cheese mixture into chocolate. Pour *remaining* cream cheese mixture over crust. Pour chocolate mixture over cream cheese mixture. Swirl mixtures with spoon, pulling plain cream cheese mixture up to surface.

Bake in preheated 325°F. oven for 40 to 45 minutes or until set. Cool in pan to room temperature on wire rack; chill until firm. Cut into squares; cut each square in half diagonally to form triangles. Makes 2½ dozen triangles.

Pictured on pages 20 and 21.

Milk Chocolate Florentine Cookies

⅔ cup butter

2 cups quick oats

1 cup granulated sugar

⅔ cup all-purpose flour

¼ cup light or dark corn syrup

¼ cup milk

1 teaspoon vanilla extract

¼ teaspoon salt

2 cups (11½-ounce package) NESTLÉ TOLL HOUSE Milk Chocolate Morsels

Melt butter in medium saucepan; remove from heat. Stir in oats, granulated sugar, flour, corn syrup, milk, vanilla and salt; mix well. Drop by level teaspoon about 3 inches apart onto foil-lined baking sheets. Spread thinly with rubber spatula.

Bake in preheated 375°F. oven for 6 to 8 minutes or until golden brown. Cool completely on baking sheets on wire racks. Peel foil from cookies.

Microwave morsels in medium, microwave-safe bowl on MEDIUM-HIGH (70%) power for 1 minute; stir. Microwave at additional 10- to 20-second intervals, stirring until smooth.

Spread thin layer of melted chocolate onto flat side of *half* the cookies. Top with *remaining* cookies, placing flat side against chocolate. Makes about 3½ dozen sandwich cookies.

Milk Chocolate
Florentine Cookies

Chocolate Gingerbread Boys and Girls

2 cups (12-ounce package) NESTLÉ TOLL HOUSE
   Semi-Sweet Chocolate Morsels, *divided*

2¾ cups all-purpose flour

1 teaspoon baking soda

½ teaspoon salt

½ teaspoon ground ginger

½ teaspoon ground cinnamon

3 tablespoons butter or margarine, softened

3 tablespoons granulated sugar

½ cup molasses

¼ cup water

   Prepared vanilla frosting or colored icing in tubes

Microwave *1½ cups* morsels in medium, microwave-safe bowl on HIGH (100%) power for 1 minute; stir. Microwave at additional 10- to 20-second intervals, stirring until smooth. Cool to room temperature.

Combine flour, baking soda, salt, ginger and cinnamon in medium bowl. Beat butter and granulated sugar in small mixer bowl until creamy. Beat in molasses and melted chocolate. Gradually add flour mixture alternately with water, beating until smooth. Cover and chill for 1 hour or until firm.

Roll *half* of dough to ¼-inch thickness on floured surface with floured rolling pin. Cut into gingerbread boys and girls, using cookie cutters or a stencil (see Cookie Art, *page 22*). Place on ungreased baking sheets. Repeat with remaining dough.

Bake in preheated 350°F. oven for 5 to 6 minutes or until edges are set but centers are still slightly soft. Let stand for 2 minutes; remove to wire racks to cool completely.

Place *remaining* morsels in heavy-duty plastic bag. Microwave on HIGH (100%) power for 45 seconds; knead. Microwave at additional 10-second intervals, kneading until smooth. Cut a small hole in corner of bag; squeeze to pipe over cookies. Decorate with piped frosting or icing. Makes 2½ dozen cookies.

Cookie Pops

1⅔ cups all-purpose flour

1 teaspoon baking soda

½ teaspoon salt

1 cup (2 sticks) butter or margarine, softened

¾ cup granulated sugar

¾ cup packed brown sugar

2 teaspoons vanilla extract

2 eggs

2 cups (12-ounce package) NESTLÉ TOLL HOUSE Semi-Sweet Chocolate Morsels

2 cups quick or old-fashioned oats

1 cup raisins

About 24 wooden craft sticks

1 container (16 ounces) prepared vanilla frosting, colored as desired

Colored icing in tubes and/or colored candies

Combine flour, baking soda and salt in small bowl. Beat butter, granulated sugar, brown sugar and vanilla in large mixer bowl until creamy. Beat in eggs, one at a time, beating well after each addition. Gradually beat in flour mixture. Stir in morsels, oats and raisins. Drop dough by level ¼-cup measure about 3 inches apart onto ungreased baking sheets. Shape into rounded mounds. Insert wooden stick into side of each mound.

Bake in preheated 325°F. oven for 14 to 18 minutes or until golden brown. Let stand for 2 minutes; remove to wire racks to cool completely. Decorate pops using colored frosting and icing and/or candies. Makes about 2 dozen cookie pops.

Chocolate Gingerbread Boys and Girls (see recipe opposite page) and Cookie Pops (see recipe above)

Chocolate Amaretto Bars

CRUST
3 cups all-purpose flour

1 cup (2 sticks) butter or margarine, cut into pieces and softened

½ cup packed brown sugar

FILLING
4 eggs

¾ cup light corn syrup

¾ cup granulated sugar

¼ cup amaretto liqueur or ½ teaspoon almond extract

2 tablespoons butter or margarine, melted

1 tablespoon cornstarch

2 cups (about 7 ounces) sliced almonds

2 cups (12-ounce package) NESTLÉ TOLL HOUSE Semi-Sweet Chocolate Morsels, *divided*

Chocolate Drizzle (optional recipe follows)

For Crust: Beat flour, butter and brown sugar in large mixer bowl until crumbly. Press into greased 13 x 9-inch baking pan. Bake in preheated 350°F. oven 12 to 15 minutes or until golden brown.

For Filling: Beat eggs, corn syrup, granulated sugar, liqueur, butter and cornstarch in medium bowl with wire whisk. Stir in almonds and *1⅔ cups* morsels. Pour and spread over hot crust.

Bake at 350°F. for 25 to 30 minutes or until center is set. Cool in pan to room temperature on wire rack. If desired, top with Chocolate Drizzle. Chill for 5 minutes or until chocolate is firm. Cut into bars. Makes 2½ dozen bars.

For Chocolate Drizzle: Place *remaining* morsels in heavy-duty plastic bag. Microwave on HIGH (100%) power for 45 seconds; knead bag to mix. Microwave at additional 10-second intervals, kneading until smooth. Cut a small hole in corner of bag; squeeze to drizzle chocolate over bars.

Chocolate Amaretto Bars

Deep Chocolate Cheesecake Bars

CRUST
1½ cups all-purpose flour
½ cup packed brown sugar
½ cup (1 stick) butter or margarine, melted

CHEESECAKE TOPPING
2 cups (12-ounce package) NESTLÉ TOLL HOUSE Semi-Sweet Chocolate Morsels

2 packages (8 ounces *each*) cream cheese, softened
⅔ cup granulated sugar
2 teaspoons vanilla extract
2 eggs
½ cup CARNATION Evaporated Milk
Sifted powdered sugar

For Crust: Combine flour, brown sugar and butter in medium bowl; press onto bottom of greased 13 x 9-inch baking pan. Bake in preheated 350°F. oven for 10 to 12 minutes or until golden brown around edges.

For Cheesecake Topping: Microwave morsels in medium, microwave-safe bowl on HIGH (100%) power for 1 minute; stir. Microwave at additional 10- to 20-second intervals, stirring until smooth. Cool to room temperature. Beat cream cheese, granulated sugar and vanilla in medium mixer bowl until smooth. Beat in eggs. Gradually beat in evaporated milk and melted chocolate. Pour over crust.

Bake in 350° F. oven for 25 to 35 minutes or until center is set. Cool in pan to room temperature on wire rack; chill until firm. Sprinkle with powdered sugar. Cut into diamonds (see Creative Cuts tip box, *page 63)* or bars. Makes 4 dozen bars.

Deep Chocolate Cheesecake Bars

Pumpkin Spiced and Iced Cookies

2¼ cups all-purpose flour

1½ teaspoons pumpkin pie spice

1 teaspoon baking powder

½ teaspoon baking soda

½ teaspoon salt

1 cup (2 sticks) butter or margarine, softened

1 cup granulated sugar

1¾ cups (15- or 16-ounce can) LIBBY'S® Solid Pack Pumpkin

2 eggs

1 teaspoon vanilla extract

2 cups (12-ounce package) NESTLÉ TOLL HOUSE Semi-Sweet Chocolate Morsels

1 cup chopped walnuts (optional)

Vanilla Glaze (recipe follows)

Combine flour, pumpkin pie spice, baking powder, baking soda and salt in medium bowl. Beat butter and granulated sugar in large mixer bowl until creamy. Beat in pumpkin, eggs and vanilla. Gradually beat in flour mixture. Stir in morsels and walnuts. Drop by rounded tablespoon onto greased baking sheets.

Bake in preheated 375°F. oven for 15 to 20 minutes or until edges are lightly browned. Let stand for 5 minutes; remove to wire racks to cool completely. Drizzle or spread with Vanilla Glaze. Makes about 5½ dozen cookies.

For Vanilla Glaze: Combine 1 cup powdered sugar, 1 to 1½ tablespoons milk and ½ teaspoon vanilla extract in small bowl; mix well.

Pumpkin Spiced and Iced Cookies

Mini Chip Snowball Cookies

1½ cups (3 sticks) butter or margarine, softened
¾ cup powdered sugar
1 tablespoon vanilla extract
½ teaspoon salt
3 cups all-purpose flour

2 cups (12-ounce package) NESTLÉ TOLL HOUSE Semi-Sweet Chocolate Mini Morsels
½ cup finely chopped nuts
Powdered sugar

Beat butter, ¾ cup powdered sugar, vanilla and salt in large mixer bowl until creamy. Gradually beat in flour. Stir in morsels and nuts. Shape level tablespoonfuls of dough into 1-inch balls. Place on ungreased baking sheets.

Bake in preheated 375°F. oven for 10 to 12 minutes or until cookies are set and lightly browned. Remove from oven. Sift sugar over hot cookies on baking sheet. Let stand for 10 minutes; remove to wire racks to cool completely. Sprinkle with additional sugar, if desired. Store in airtight containers. Makes about 5 dozen cookies.

Double Chocolate Peanut Butter Thumbprint Cookies (see recipe opposite page) and Mini Chip Snowball Cookies (see recipe above)

Double Chocolate Peanut Butter Thumbprint Cookies

1½ cups all-purpose flour

⅓ cup NESTLÉ TOLL HOUSE Baking Cocoa

1½ teaspoons baking powder

¼ teaspoon salt

2 cups (12-ounce package) NESTLÉ TOLL HOUSE Semi-Sweet Chocolate Morsels, *divided*

1 cup granulated sugar

About 1 cup chunky or creamy peanut butter (not all-natural), *divided*

⅓ cup butter or margarine, softened

1½ teaspoons vanilla extract

2 eggs

Combine flour, cocoa, baking powder and salt in small bowl. Melt *1 cup* morsels in small, *heavy* saucepan over *lowest possible* heat, stirring constantly until smooth.

Beat granulated sugar, *⅓ cup* peanut butter, butter and vanilla in large mixer bowl until creamy. Beat in melted chocolate. Add eggs, one at a time, beating well after each addition. Gradually beat in flour mixture. Stir in *remaining* morsels. Cover; chill just until firm.

Shape dough into 1½-inch balls. Place on ungreased baking sheets. Press ½-inch deep centers with thumb. Fill each center with about *½ teaspoon* peanut butter.

Bake in preheated 350°F. oven for 10 to 15 minutes or until sides are set but centers are still slightly soft. Let stand for 2 minutes; remove to wire racks to cool completely. Makes about 3½ dozen.

Cookie Ja

Milk Chocolate Oatmeal Cookies (see recipe opposite page),
Frosted Maple Pecan White Chip Cookies (see recipe, page 40)
and Chocolate Peanut Cookies (see recipe, page 45)

Treasures

Many a cherished memory is captured in that cookie jar on the counter, where little hands reached in again and again for just one more irresistible treat. When it comes to cookies, who needs to grow up? Bake new memories for your family, choosing from this assortment of homespun drop cookies. With goodies this tasty, they won't stay in the cookie jar for long!

Milk Chocolate Oatmeal Cookies

1¼ cups all-purpose flour
½ teaspoon baking powder
½ teaspoon baking soda
½ teaspoon ground cinnamon
¼ teaspoon salt
¾ cup (1½ sticks) butter or margarine, softened
¾ cup packed brown sugar

⅓ cup granulated sugar
1½ teaspoons vanilla extract
1 egg
2 tablespoons milk
2 cups (11½-ounce package) NESTLÉ TOLL HOUSE Milk Chocolate Morsels
1 cup quick or old-fashioned oats
½ cup raisins (optional)

Combine flour, baking powder, baking soda, cinnamon and salt in small bowl. Beat butter, brown sugar, granulated sugar and vanilla in large mixer bowl until creamy. Beat in egg. Gradually beat in flour mixture and milk. Stir in morsels, oats and raisins. Drop by rounded tablespoon onto ungreased baking sheets.

Bake in preheated 375°F. oven for 10 to 14 minutes or until edges are crisp but centers are still soft. Let stand for 2 minutes; remove to wire racks to cool completely. Makes about 3 dozen.

Frosted Maple Pecan White Chip Cookies

3 cups all-purpose flour

2 teaspoons baking soda

2 cups packed brown sugar

1 cup shortening

½ cup (1 stick) butter or margarine, softened

2 eggs

1 teaspoon maple flavoring

1 teaspoon vanilla extract

2 cups (12-ounce package) NESTLÉ TOLL HOUSE Premier White Morsels

½ cup chopped pecans

Maple Frosting (recipe follows)

About 60 pecan halves (3½ to 4 ounces)

Combine flour and baking soda in medium bowl. Beat brown sugar, shortening, butter, eggs, maple flavoring and vanilla in large mixer bowl until creamy. Gradually beat in flour mixture. Stir in morsels and chopped pecans. Drop by rounded tablespoon onto ungreased baking sheets.

Bake in preheated 350°F. oven for 9 to 12 minutes or until light golden brown. Let stand for 2 minutes; remove to wire racks to cool completely. Spread with Maple Frosting; top each cookie with pecan half. Makes about 5 dozen cookies.

For Maple Frosting: Combine 4 cups powdered sugar, 4 to 6 tablespoons milk, ¼ cup softened butter and 1 teaspoon maple flavoring in medium bowl; stir until smooth.

Pictured on pages 38 and 39.

Butterscotch Apple Cookies

2½ cups all-purpose flour

2 teaspoons ground cinnamon

1 teaspoon baking soda

½ teaspoon salt

1⅓ cups packed brown sugar

½ cup (1 stick) butter or margarine, softened

1 egg

½ cup apple juice

1⅔ cups (11-ounce package) NESTLÉ TOLL HOUSE Butterscotch Flavored Morsels, *divided*

¾ cup (1 small) unpeeled grated apple

¾ cup chopped walnuts, *divided*

Butterscotch Glaze (recipe follows)

Combine flour, cinnamon, baking soda and salt in medium bowl. Beat brown sugar and butter in large mixer bowl until creamy. Beat in egg. Gradually beat in flour mixture alternately with apple juice. Stir in *1⅓ cups* morsels, apple and *½ cup* walnuts. Drop by slightly rounded tablespoon onto lightly greased baking sheets.

Bake in preheated 350°F. oven for 10 to 12 minutes or until lightly browned. Let stand for 2 minutes; remove to wire racks to cool completely. Spread with Butterscotch Glaze; sprinkle with *remaining* walnuts. Makes about 3½ dozen cookies.

For Butterscotch Glaze: Melt *remaining* morsels and 2 tablespoons butter in small, *heavy* saucepan over *lowest possible* heat. Remove from heat; stir in 1 cup sifted powdered sugar and 1 to 1½ tablespoons apple juice until smooth.

Butterscotch Apple Cookies

Giant Decorated Chocolate Chip Cookies

2 cups all-purpose flour	2 cups (11½-ounce package) NESTLÉ TOLL HOUSE Milk Chocolate Morsels, *divided*
1 teaspoon baking soda	1 cup chopped nuts
¼ teaspoon salt	1 cup raisins
1¼ cups packed brown sugar	2 containers (16 ounces *each*) prepared vanilla frosting
1 cup (2 sticks) butter or margarine, softened	Colored icing in tubes
1 teaspoon vanilla extract	Assorted candy
1 egg	

Combine flour, baking soda and salt in small bowl. Beat brown sugar, butter and vanilla in large mixer bowl until creamy. Beat in egg. Gradually beat in flour mixture. Stir in *1½ cups* morsels, nuts and raisins. Drop *½ cup* dough onto ungreased baking sheet; spread to 4-inch circle. Repeat with remaining dough.

Bake in preheated 375°F. oven for 10 to 12 minutes or until edges are golden brown. Let stand for 5 minutes; remove to wire racks to cool completely.

Decorate cookies with frosting, *remaining* morsels, icing and assorted candy, if desired. Makes 10 large cookies.

Giant Decorated Chocolate Chip Cookies

Crispy Polynesian Butterscotch Cookies

1½ cups all-purpose flour	1 teaspoon vanilla extract
½ teaspoon baking soda	1⅔ cups (11-ounce package) NESTLÉ TOLL HOUSE Butterscotch Flavored Morsels
½ teaspoon salt	½ cup quick oats
½ cup butter or margarine, softened	½ cup crushed cereal flakes
½ cup vegetable oil	½ cup flaked coconut
½ cup granulated sugar	½ cup chopped nuts
½ cup packed brown sugar	
1 egg	

Combine flour, baking soda and salt in small bowl. Beat butter, oil, granulated sugar, brown sugar, egg and vanilla in large mixer bowl until creamy. Gradually beat in flour mixture. Stir in morsels, oats, crushed cereal, coconut and nuts. Drop by rounded tablespoon onto ungreased baking sheets.

Bake in preheated 350°F. oven for 10 to 14 minutes or until edges are crisp but centers are still slightly soft. Let stand for 2 minutes; remove to wire racks to cool. Makes 3½ dozen cookies.

Pictured on page 47.

10 Tips for Best-Ever Cookies

1. Baking sheets and pans of shiny, heavy-gauge aluminum will bake cookies and bars more evenly than thin, dark metal or glass pans. Choose baking sheets that are the right size for your oven, allowing at least 2 inches of space between the sides of the baking sheet and the oven walls or door.

2. Grease baking sheets only when a recipe recommends it. Some cookies will spread too much if the sheet is greased. When the recipe calls for ungreased baking sheets, cool and wash them between batches of cookies.

3. To prevent cookies from spreading too much on warm or humid days, spoon cookie dough onto baking sheets, then chill for a few minutes before baking.

4. For evenly shaped cookies, try a scoop. When a recipe calls for rounded tablespoons of dough, use a 1½-inch diameter scoop with dough leveled.

5. Butter and regular stick margarine work best for the recipes in this book. Also, all of the recipes were tested using large eggs.

Chocolate Peanut Cookies

2 bars (2 ounces *each*) NESTLÉ TOLL HOUSE Semi-
   Sweet Baking Chocolate, broken into pieces
1¼ cups all-purpose flour
¾ teaspoon baking soda
½ teaspoon salt
½ cup (1 stick) butter or margarine, softened

½ cup packed brown sugar
¼ cup granulated sugar
2 teaspoons vanilla extract
1 egg
1½ cups coarsely chopped honey-roasted peanuts

Microwave baking bars in small, microwave-safe bowl on HIGH (100%) power for 1 minute; stir. Microwave at additional 10- to 20-second intervals, stirring until smooth; cool.

Combine flour, baking soda and salt in small bowl. Beat butter, brown sugar, granulated sugar and vanilla in large mixer bowl. Beat in melted chocolate and egg. Gradually beat in flour mixture. Stir in peanuts. Drop by rounded tablespoon onto ungreased baking sheets.

Bake in preheated 375°F. oven for 8 to 9 minutes or until edges are set but centers are still slightly soft. Let stand for 3 minutes; remove to wire racks to cool completely. Makes 2½ dozen cookies.

Pictured on pages 38 and 39.

6. When baking bars and brownies, lining the pan with heavy-duty aluminum foil makes them easier to remove from the pan. Cool completely, then lift out and peel the foil away. Using foil also makes the pan easier to clean.

7. To achieve the right oven temperature before baking, preheat your oven for about 10 minutes.

8. Bake cookies or brownies on the middle rack of the oven, one pan at a time, to prevent over-darkened bottoms and uncooked tops.

9. Check cookies and bars for doneness at the minimum baking time stated in the recipe. Remember, cookies continue to bake slightly after they are removed from the oven. For chewy cookies, take them out while they are still on the lighter side.

10. Let most cookies stand on the baking sheet for 1 or 2 minutes (or as long as directed in recipe) to continue cooking and to become firm enough to remove from the baking sheets. Then, transfer cookies to wire racks.

White Chip Orange Cookies

2¼ cups all-purpose flour

¾ teaspoon baking soda

½ teaspoon salt

1 cup butter or margarine, softened

½ cup granulated sugar

½ cup packed light brown sugar

1 egg

2 to 3 teaspoons grated orange peel

2 cups (12-ounce package) NESTLÉ TOLL HOUSE Premier White Morsels

Combine flour, baking soda and salt in small bowl. Beat butter, granulated sugar and brown sugar in large mixer bowl until creamy. Beat in egg and orange peel. Gradually beat in flour mixture. Stir in morsels. Drop dough by rounded tablespoon onto ungreased baking sheets. Bake in preheated 350°F. oven for 10 to 12 minutes or until edges are light golden brown. Let stand for 2 minutes; remove to racks to cool completely. Makes 39 cookies.

Double Chocolate Dream Cookies

2¼ cups all-purpose flour

½ cup NESTLÉ TOLL HOUSE Baking Cocoa

1 teaspoon baking soda

½ teaspoon salt

1 cup butter or margarine, softened

1 cup packed brown sugar

¾ cup granulated sugar

1 teaspoon vanilla extract

2 eggs

2 cups (12-ounce package) NESTLÉ TOLL HOUSE Semi-Sweet Chocolate Morsels

Combine flour, cocoa, baking soda and salt in small bowl. Beat butter, brown sugar, granulated sugar and vanilla in mixer bowl until creamy. Beat in eggs about 2 minutes or until light and fluffy. Gradually beat in flour mixture. Stir in morsels. Drop by rounded tablespoon onto ungreased baking sheets. Bake in preheated 375°F. oven 8 to 10 minutes or until puffed. Let stand for 2 minutes; remove to wire racks to cool completely. Makes 4½ dozen cookies.

White Chip Orange Cookies, Double Chocolate Dream Cookies and Crispy Polynesian Butterscotch Cookies (see recipe, page 44)

Island Cookies

1⅔ cups all-purpose flour

¾ teaspoon baking powder

½ teaspoon baking soda

½ teaspoon salt

¾ cup (1½ sticks) butter or margarine, softened

¾ cup packed brown sugar

⅓ cup granulated sugar

1 teaspoon vanilla extract

1 egg

2 cups (11½-ounce package) NESTLÉ TOLL HOUSE Milk Chocolate Morsels*

1 cup flaked coconut, toasted if desired

¾ cup macadamia nuts or walnuts, chopped

Combine flour, baking powder, baking soda and salt in small bowl. Beat butter, brown sugar, granulated sugar and vanilla in large mixer bowl until creamy. Beat in egg. Gradually beat in flour mixture. Stir in morsels, coconut and nuts. Drop by slightly rounded tablespoon onto ungreased baking sheets.

Bake in preheated 375°F. oven for 8 to 11 minutes or until edges are lightly browned. Let stand for 2 minutes; remove to wire racks to cool completely. Makes about 3 dozen cookies.

*Note: NESTLÉ TOLL HOUSE Semi-Sweet Chocolate Morsels, Semi-Sweet Chocolate Mini Morsels, Mint-Chocolate Morsels, Premier White Morsels or Butterscotch Flavored Morsels may be substituted for the Milk Chocolate Morsels.

Island Cookies

Chocolate Mint Brownie Cookies

1½ cups (10-ounce package) NESTLÉ TOLL HOUSE
    Mint-Chocolate Morsels, *divided*

1¾ cups all-purpose flour

½ teaspoon baking soda

¼ teaspoon salt

½ cup (1 stick) butter or margarine, softened

½ cup granulated sugar

¼ cup packed brown sugar

1 teaspoon vanilla extract

2 eggs

¾ cup chopped nuts

Melt ¾ *cup* morsels in small, *heavy* saucepan over *lowest possible* heat. When morsels begin to melt, remove from heat; stir. Return to heat for a few seconds at a time, stirring until smooth. Cool to room temperature.

Combine flour, baking soda and salt in small bowl. Beat butter, granulated sugar, brown sugar and vanilla in large mixer bowl until creamy. Add eggs, one at a time, beating well after each addition. Beat in melted chocolate. Gradually beat in flour mixture. Stir in *remaining* morsels and nuts. Drop dough by rounded tablespoon onto ungreased baking sheets.

Bake in preheated 350°F. oven for 8 to 12 minutes or until sides are set but centers are still soft. Let stand for 2 minutes; remove to wire racks to cool completely. Makes about 3 dozen cookies.

Pictured on page 51.

Macadamia Nut White Chip Pumpkin Cookies

2 cups all-purpose flour

2 teaspoons ground cinnamon

1 teaspoon ground cardamom

1 teaspoon baking soda

1 cup (2 sticks) butter or margarine, softened

½ cup granulated sugar

½ cup packed brown sugar

1 cup LIBBY'S® Solid Pack Pumpkin

1 egg

2 teaspoons vanilla extract

2 cups (12-ounce package) NESTLÉ TOLL HOUSE Premier White Morsels

⅔ cup coarsely chopped macadamia nuts or walnuts, toasted

Combine flour, cinnamon, cardamom and baking soda in small bowl. Beat butter, granulated sugar and brown sugar in large mixer bowl until creamy. Beat in pumpkin, egg and vanilla until well mixed. Gradually beat in flour mixture. Stir in morsels and macadamia nuts. Drop by rounded tablespoon onto greased baking sheets; flatten slightly with back of spoon or greased bottom of glass dipped into granulated sugar.

Bake in preheated 350°F. oven for 11 to 14 minutes or until centers are set. Cool for 2 minutes; remove to wire racks to cool completely. Makes about 4 dozen cookies.

*Chocolate Mint Brownie Cookies
(see recipe, page 49) and Macadamia
Nut White Chip Pumpkin Cookies
(see recipe above)*

Family-Pleasi

For afternoon snacktime, potluck gatherings, or for any occasion, bar cookies and brownies are perennially popular. Each of these rich, chocolaty recipes mixes together easily from everyday ingredients, leaving plenty of time to enjoy the scrumptious results. Treat loved ones to pleasure by the panful with this medley of tried-and-true Nestlé Toll House goodies.

Bar Cookies

Left to right: Butterscotch Cream Cheese Bars (see recipe, page 54), Chocolate Peanut Butter Bars (see recipe, page 55) and Black Forest Brownie Squares (see recipe, page 55)

Butterscotch Cream Cheese Bars

1⅔ cups (11-ounce package) NESTLÉ TOLL HOUSE Butterscotch Flavored Morsels

6 tablespoons (¾ stick) butter or margarine

2 cups graham cracker crumbs

2 cups chopped walnuts

2 packages (8 ounces *each*) cream cheese, softened

½ cup granulated sugar

4 eggs

¼ cup all-purpose flour

2 tablespoons lemon juice

Melt morsels and butter in medium, *heavy* saucepan over *lowest possible* heat, stirring constantly until smooth. Stir in crumbs and walnuts. Reserve *2 cups* crumb mixture for topping; press *remaining* mixture into ungreased 15 x 10-inch jelly-roll pan. Bake in preheated 350°F. oven for 12 minutes.

Beat cream cheese and granulated sugar in large mixer bowl until creamy. Add eggs, one at a time, beating well after each addition. Gradually beat in flour and lemon juice. Pour over crust; sprinkle with reserved crumb mixture.

Bake at 350° F. for 20 to 25 minutes or until set. Cool completely in pan on wire rack. Cut into diamonds (see Creative Cuts tip box, *page 63*) or bars; chill. Makes 4 dozen bars.

Pictured on pages 52 and 53.

Black Forest Brownie Squares

2 cups (12-ounce package) NESTLÉ TOLL HOUSE Semi-Sweet Chocolate Morsels, *divided*

½ cup butter or margarine, cut into pieces

3 eggs

1¼ cups all-purpose flour

1 cup granulated sugar

1 teaspoon vanilla extract

¼ teaspoon baking soda

1½ cups frozen whipped topping, thawed

2 cups (21-ounce can) cherry pie filling or topping

Melt *1 cup* morsels and butter in large, *heavy* saucepan over *lowest possible* heat, stirring until smooth. Remove from heat; stir in eggs. Gradually stir in flour, granulated sugar, vanilla and baking soda. Stir in *remaining* morsels. Spread into greased 13 x 9-inch baking pan.

Bake in preheated 350°F. oven for 20 to 25 minutes or until wooden pick inserted in center comes out slightly sticky. Cool completely in pan on wire rack. Spread with whipped topping. Top with pie filling. Cut into squares. Makes 24 squares.

Chocolate Peanut Butter Bars

1¾ cups all-purpose flour

½ teaspoon baking soda

1¼ cups granulated sugar

¾ cup creamy or chunky peanut butter

½ cup butter or margarine, softened

1 teaspoon vanilla extract

1 egg

2 cups (12-ounce package) NESTLÉ TOLL HOUSE Semi-Sweet Chocolate Morsels, *divided*

Combine flour and baking soda in small bowl. Beat granulated sugar, peanut butter, butter and vanilla in large mixer bowl until creamy. Beat in egg. Gradually beat in flour mixture. Stir in *1¼ cups* morsels. Press into ungreased 13 x 9-inch baking pan. Sprinkle with *remaining* morsels; press down slightly.

Bake in preheated 350°F. oven for 20 to 25 minutes or until center is set. Cool completely in pan on wire rack. Chill for a few minutes. Cut into bars. Makes 3 dozen bars.

Recipes pictured on pages 52 and 53.

Fruit and Chocolate Dream Bars

CRUST

1¼ cups all-purpose flour

½ cup granulated sugar

½ cup (1 stick) butter or margarine

TOPPING

⅔ cup all-purpose flour

½ cup chopped pecans

⅓ cup packed brown sugar

6 tablespoons (¾ stick) butter or margarine, softened

½ cup raspberry or strawberry jam

2 cups (11½-ounce package) NESTLÉ TOLL HOUSE Milk Chocolate Morsels

For Crust: Combine flour and granulated sugar in medium bowl. Cut in butter with pastry blender or 2 knives until mixture resembles coarse crumbs. Press onto bottom of greased 9-inch square baking pan. Bake in preheated 375°F. oven for 18 to 22 minutes or until set but not brown.

For Topping: Combine flour, pecans and brown sugar in same bowl. Cut in butter with pastry blender or 2 knives until mixture resembles coarse crumbs.

Spread jam over hot crust. Sprinkle with topping and morsels. Bake at 375° F. for 15 to 20 minutes or until golden brown. Cool completely in pan on wire rack. Cut into bars. Makes 2½ dozen bars.

Fruit and Chocolate
Dream Bars

Fudgy Peanut Butter Bars

CRUST

- 1½ cups all-purpose flour
- ¾ cup finely chopped dry roasted peanuts
- ½ cup packed brown sugar
- ½ cup (1 stick) butter or margarine, melted

TOPPING

- 2 cups (12-ounce package) NESTLÉ TOLL HOUSE Semi-Sweet Chocolate Morsels
- ¾ cup creamy or chunky peanut butter
- ⅓ cup sifted powdered sugar

For Crust: Combine flour, peanuts, brown sugar and butter in ungreased 13 x 9-inch baking pan; press onto bottom of pan. Bake in preheated 350°F. oven for 10 to 12 minutes or until light brown around edges.

For Topping: Microwave morsels and peanut butter in medium, microwave-safe bowl on HIGH (100%) power for 1 minute; stir. Microwave at additional 10- to 20-second intervals, stirring until smooth. Add powdered sugar; stir vigorously until smooth. Spread over hot cookie base. Chill just until chocolate is no longer shiny. Cut into bars. Serve at room temperature. Makes 3 dozen bars.

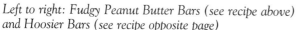
Left to right: Fudgy Peanut Butter Bars (see recipe above) and Hoosier Bars (see recipe opposite page)

Hoosier Bars

1½ cups all-purpose flour
1 teaspoon baking soda
1 cup packed brown sugar, *divided*
½ cup granulated sugar
½ cup (1 stick) butter or margarine, softened

2 eggs, separated
1 teaspoon vanilla extract
2 cups (12-ounce package) NESTLÉ TOLL HOUSE Semi-Sweet Chocolate Morsels, *divided*
¾ cup honey-roasted peanuts, *divided*

Combine flour and baking soda in small bowl. Beat ½ *cup* brown sugar, granulated sugar and butter in large mixer bowl until creamy. Beat in egg yolks and vanilla. Gradually beat in flour mixture until crumbly. Stir in *1½ cups* morsels and ½ *cup* peanuts. Press onto bottom of greased 13 x 9-inch baking pan.

Beat egg whites in small mixer bowl until soft peaks form. Gradually beat in *remaining* brown sugar until stiff peaks form (see photo and tip, *page 14*); spread mixture over dough. Sprinkle with *remaining* morsels and *remaining* peanuts.

Bake in preheated 325°F. oven for 35 to 40 minutes or until top is set and lightly browned. Cool in pan on wire rack for 20 minutes. Cut into bars while still warm. Makes 3 dozen bars.

Chocolate Macaroon Bars

1 package (18¼ ounces) chocolate cake mix
⅓ cup butter or margarine, softened
2 eggs, *divided*
1¼ cups (14-ounce can) CARNATION Sweetened Condensed Milk

1 teaspoon vanilla extract
2 cups (12-ounce package) NESTLÉ TOLL HOUSE Semi-Sweet Chocolate Morsels
1⅓ cups flaked coconut, *divided*
¾ cup chopped nuts (optional)

Beat cake mix, butter and *1 egg* in large mixer bowl until mixture is crumbly. Firmly press onto bottom of greased 13 x 9-inch baking pan.

Combine sweetened condensed milk, *remaining* egg and vanilla in medium bowl; stir in morsels, *1 cup* coconut and nuts. Spread over mixture in baking pan. Sprinkle with *remaining* coconut.

Bake in preheated 350°F. oven for 30 to 40 minutes or until golden brown (center will set when cooled). Cool completely in pan on wire rack. Cut into bars. Makes 2½ dozen bars.

Right: Craggy-Topped Fudge Brownies (see recipe, page 63),
left: Chocolate Macaroon Bars (see recipe above),
top: Moist and Minty Brownies (see recipe, page 62)

Moist and Minty Brownies

BROWNIES
- 1¼ cups all-purpose flour
- ½ teaspoon baking soda
- ¼ teaspoon salt
- ¾ cup granulated sugar
- ½ cup (1 stick) butter or margarine
- 2 tablespoons water
- 1½ cups (10-ounce package) NESTLÉ TOLL HOUSE Mint-Chocolate Morsels, *divided*
- 1 teaspoon vanilla extract
- 2 eggs

FROSTING
- 1 container (16 ounces) prepared vanilla frosting
- 1 tube (4¼ ounces) chocolate decorating icing

For Brownies: Combine flour, baking soda and salt in small bowl. Combine sugar, butter and water in medium saucepan. Bring *just to a boil* over medium heat, stirring constantly; remove from heat. (Or, combine granulated sugar, butter and water in medium, microwave-safe bowl. Microwave on HIGH [100%] power for 3 minutes, stirring halfway through cooking time. Stir until smooth.)

Add *1 cup* morsels and vanilla; stir until smooth. Add eggs, one at a time, stirring well after each addition. Stir in flour mixture and *remaining* morsels. Spread into greased 9-inch square baking pan.

Bake in preheated 350°F. oven for 20 to 30 minutes or until center is set. Cool completely (center will sink) in pan on rack.

For Frosting: Spread vanilla frosting over brownies. Squeeze chocolate icing in parallel lines over frosting. Drag wooden pick through chocolate icing to feather. Let stand until frosting is set. Cut into bars. Makes 16 brownies.

Pictured on page 61.

Craggy-Topped Fudge Brownies

1 cup granulated sugar
½ cup (1 stick) butter or margarine
2 cups (12-ounce package) NESTLÉ TOLL HOUSE
    Semi-Sweet Chocolate Morsels, *divided*
3 eggs

1⅓ cups all-purpose flour
1 teaspoon vanilla extract
¼ teaspoon baking soda
⅓ cup chopped nuts

Heat granulated sugar and butter in medium saucepan over low heat, stirring until butter is melted. Remove from heat. Add *1¼ cups* morsels; stir until melted. Stir in eggs. Stir in flour, vanilla and baking soda until combined. Spread into greased 13 x 9-inch baking pan.

Bake in preheated 350°F. oven for 18 to 22 minutes or until wooden pick inserted in center comes out slightly sticky.

Creative Cuts

For a creative flair with cookies and brownies, cut them into shapes other than the standard rectangles and squares. To make triangles, cut bars into 3-inch squares, then cut each square in half diagonally. For diamonds, cut parallel lines 2 inches apart across the length of the pan, then cut diagonal lines 2 inches apart. For extra fun, cut brownies and bars (choose less-crumbly bars) with cookie cutters.

Sprinkle with *remaining* morsels and nuts while still hot. Cover with foil; chill in pan until completely cooled. Cut into bars.
Makes 2 dozen brownies.

Pictured on page 61.

White Chip Meringue Dessert Squares

CRUST

 2 cups all-purpose flour
½ cup powdered sugar
 1 cup (2 sticks) butter or margarine, softened

TOPPING

 2 cups (12-ounce package) NESTLÉ TOLL HOUSE Premier White Morsels
1¼ cups sliced or chopped nuts, *divided*
 3 egg whites
 1 cup packed brown sugar

For Crust: Combine flour and powdered sugar in a medium bowl. Cut in butter with pastry blender or 2 knives until mixture resembles coarse crumbs. Press onto bottom of ungreased 13 x 9-inch baking pan. Bake in preheated 375°F. oven for 10 to 12 minutes or until set.

For Topping: Sprinkle morsels and *1 cup* nuts over hot crust. Beat egg whites in small mixer bowl until frothy. Gradually add brown sugar. Beat until stiff peaks form (see photo and tip, *page 14*). Gently spread egg white mixture over morsels and nuts. Sprinkle with *remaining* nuts.

Bake at 375° F. for 15 to 20 minutes or until golden brown. Serve warm or cool. Cut into bars. Makes 2 dozen squares.

This page: White Chip Meringue Dessert Squares (see recipe above); opposite page: Frosted Brownies (see recipe opposite page)

Frosted Brownies

BROWNIES

- ⅔ cup all-purpose flour
- ½ teaspoon baking powder
- ¼ teaspoon salt
- 1 cup granulated sugar
- ½ cup (1 stick) butter or margarine, softened
- 2 eggs
- 3 envelopes (1 ounce *each*) NESTLÉ TOLL HOUSE Choco Bake Unsweetened Chocolate Flavor
- 1 teaspoon vanilla extract
- ½ cup chopped nuts

FUDGE FROSTING

- 3 tablespoons butter or margarine, softened
- 1 envelope (1 ounce) NESTLÉ TOLL HOUSE Choco Bake Unsweetened Chocolate Flavor
- 2 teaspoons milk
- ½ teaspoon vanilla extract
- 1 cup sifted powdered sugar

For Brownies: Combine flour, baking powder and salt in small bowl. Beat granulated sugar, butter, eggs, Choco Bake and vanilla in small mixer bowl until creamy. Gradually beat in flour mixture. Stir in nuts. Spread into greased 8-inch square baking pan.

Bake in preheated 350°F. oven for 25 to 30 minutes or until wooden pick inserted in center comes out slightly sticky. Cool completely in pan on wire rack.

For Fudge Frosting: Beat butter, Choco Bake, milk and vanilla in small mixer bowl until well blended. Gradually beat in powdered sugar until creamy. Spread onto brownies. Cut into bars. Makes 16 brownies.

Chocolate Walnut Pie Bars

CRUST

1½ cups all-purpose flour

½ cup (1 stick) butter or margarine, softened

¼ cup packed brown sugar

FILLING

3 eggs

¾ cup light corn syrup

¾ cup granulated sugar

2 tablespoons butter or margarine, melted

1 teaspoon vanilla extract

2 cups (12-ounce package) NESTLÉ TOLL HOUSE Semi-Sweet Chocolate Morsels

1½ cups coarsely chopped DIAMOND Walnuts

For Crust: Beat flour, butter and brown sugar in small mixer bowl until crumbly. Press onto bottom of greased 13 x 9-inch baking pan. Bake in preheated 350°F. oven for 12 to 15 minutes or until lightly browned.

For Filling: Beat together eggs, corn syrup, granulated sugar, butter and vanilla in large mixer bowl. Stir in morsels and walnuts; pour over hot crust.

Bake at 350° F. for 25 to 30 minutes or until center is set. Cool completely in pan on wire rack. Cut into bars. Makes 3 dozen bars.

Pictured on page 68.

Chocolate Cinnamon Nut Bars

COOKIE CRUST

- 2 cups all-purpose flour
- ¾ cup (1½ sticks) butter or margarine, softened
- ⅓ cup granulated sugar
- ¾ teaspoon baking powder
- ¾ teaspoon ground cinnamon
- 1½ cups chopped nuts

CHOCOLATE LAYER

- 1 cup (6 ounces) NESTLÉ TOLL HOUSE Semi-Sweet Chocolate Morsels
- ¼ cup (½ stick) butter or margarine, cut into pieces
- 1¼ cups packed light brown sugar
- 3 eggs
- 1 teaspoon vanilla extract
- Sifted powdered sugar

For Cookie Crust: Beat flour, butter, granulated sugar, baking powder and cinnamon in large mixer bowl until mixture is crumbly. Stir in nuts. Press onto bottom of ungreased 13 x 9-inch baking pan. Bake in preheated 350°F. oven for 15 to 18 minutes or until firm.

For Chocolate Layer: Melt morsels and butter in medium, *heavy* saucepan over *lowest possible* heat, stirring constantly until smooth. Remove from heat; stir in brown sugar, eggs and vanilla. Pour over hot crust.

Bake at 350° F. for 20 to 25 minutes or until center is set. Cool completely in pan on wire rack. Sprinkle with powdered sugar. Cut into bars. Makes 2½ dozen bars.

Pictured on page 68.

White Chip Brownies

1 cup all-purpose flour
½ cup NESTLÉ TOLL HOUSE Baking Cocoa
¾ teaspoon baking powder
¼ teaspoon salt
1¼ cups granulated sugar

¾ cup (1½ sticks) butter or margarine, melted
2 teaspoons vanilla extract
3 eggs
2 cups (12-ounce package) NESTLÉ TOLL HOUSE Premier White Morsels, *divided*

Combine flour, cocoa, baking powder and salt in medium bowl. Beat granulated sugar, butter and vanilla together in large mixer bowl until creamy. Add eggs, one at a time, beating well after each addition. Gradually beat in flour mixture. Stir in *1½ cups* morsels. Pour into greased 9-inch square baking pan.

Bake in preheated 350°F. oven for 25 to 30 minutes or until wooden pick inserted in center comes out slightly sticky. Cool completely (center will sink) in pan on wire rack.

Place *remaining* morsels in heavy-duty plastic bag. Microwave on MEDIUM-HIGH (70%) power for 45 seconds; knead bag to mix. Microwave at additional 10- to 20-second intervals, kneading until smooth. Cut a small hole in corner of bag; squeeze to drizzle over brownies. Chill for 5 minutes or until drizzle is firm. Cut into bars. Makes 16 brownies.

Dazzle with a Drizzle

A drizzle of white "chocolate" adds a pastry-shop touch to cookies, brownies, cakes, fudge and truffles. Place ½ cup NESTLÉ TOLL HOUSE Premier White Morsels or 2 bars (2 ounces *each*) NESTLÉ TOLL HOUSE Premier White Baking Bar in a heavy-duty plastic bag, and microwave as in the recipe on this page. (Semi-sweet chocolate morsels and baking bars may be melted in the same way, using HIGH power.) For a thicker or thinner drizzle, adjust the size of the hole you cut in the bag.

Top to bottom: White Chip Brownies (see recipe above), Chocolate Cinnamon Nut Bars (see recipe, page 67) and Chocolate Walnut Pie Bars (see recipe, page 66)

German Chocolate Brownies

1 package (18½ ounces) chocolate cake mix
1 cup chopped nuts
½ cup (1 stick) butter or margarine, melted

1 cup CARNATION Evaporated Milk, *divided*
35 (10-ounce package) caramels
2 cups (12-ounce package) NESTLÉ TOLL HOUSE Semi-Sweet Chocolate Morsels

Combine cake mix and nuts in large bowl. Stir in butter. Stir in *⅔ cup* evaporated milk (batter will be thick). Spread *half* of batter into ungreased 13 x 9-inch baking pan. Bake in preheated 350°F. oven for 15 minutes.

Cook caramels and *remaining* evaporated milk in small saucepan over low heat, stirring constantly until caramels are melted. Sprinkle morsels over hot base; drizzle with caramel mixture.

Drop *remaining* batter by heaping teaspoon over caramel mixture. Bake at 350° F. for 25 to 30 minutes or until center is set. Cool completely in pan on rack. Cut into bars. Makes 4 dozen.

German Chocolate Brownies

Double Espresso Brownies

ESPRESSO BROWNIES

1 cup all-purpose flour

½ teaspoon baking powder

¼ teaspoon salt

⅓ cup hot water

1 tablespoon instant espresso powder or instant coffee crystals

1 cup granulated sugar

½ cup (1 stick) butter or margarine

2 cups (12-ounce package) NESTLÉ TOLL HOUSE Semi-Sweet Chocolate Morsels, *divided*

3 eggs

ESPRESSO FROSTING

½ cup whipping cream

1 teaspoon instant espresso powder or instant coffee crystals

½ cup sifted powdered sugar

For Espresso Brownies: Combine flour, baking powder and salt in small bowl. Heat water and espresso in medium saucepan over low heat, stirring to dissolve espresso. Add granulated sugar and butter; cook, stirring constantly, until mixture comes to a boil. Remove from heat; stir in *1 cup* morsels until smooth. Add eggs, one at a time, stirring well after each addition. Stir in flour mixture. Pour into greased 9-inch square baking pan.

Bake in preheated 350°F. oven for 25 to 30 minutes or until wooden pick inserted in center comes out slightly sticky. Cool completely in pan on wire rack.

For Espresso Frosting: Heat cream and espresso in small, *heavy* saucepan over low heat, stirring to dissolve espresso. Add *remaining* morsels, stirring until smooth. Remove from heat; stir in powdered sugar. Chill until frosting is of spreading consistency. Spread onto brownies. Cut into squares. Makes 3 dozen brownies.

Double Espresso Brownies

Banana Bars

2 cups all-purpose flour
2 teaspoons baking powder
½ teaspoon salt
¾ cup (1½ sticks) butter or margarine, softened
⅔ cup granulated sugar
⅔ cup packed brown sugar

1 teaspoon vanilla extract
1 cup (2 bananas) mashed ripe banana
1 egg
2 cups (12-ounce package) NESTLÉ TOLL HOUSE Semi-Sweet Chocolate Mini Morsels
Sifted powdered sugar

Combine flour, baking powder and salt in medium bowl. Beat butter, granulated sugar, brown sugar and vanilla in large mixer bowl until creamy. Beat in bananas and egg. Gradually beat in flour mixture. Stir in morsels. Spread into greased 15 x 10-inch jelly-roll pan.

Bake in preheated 350°F. oven for 20 to 30 minutes or until wooden pick inserted in center comes out clean. Cool completely in pan on wire rack. Sprinkle with powdered sugar. Cut into bars.
Makes 6 dozen bars.

Banana Bars

Chocolate Oatmeal Bars

1 cup all-purpose flour
½ teaspoon ground cinnamon
1 cup (2 sticks) butter or margarine, softened
½ cup granulated sugar
½ cup packed brown sugar
1½ teaspoons vanilla extract

1 egg
1¼ cups quick or old-fashioned oats
2 cups (11½-ounce package) NESTLÉ TOLL HOUSE Milk Chocolate Morsels, *divided*
¾ cup finely chopped DIAMOND Walnuts, *divided*

Combine flour and cinnamon in small bowl. Beat butter, granulated sugar, brown sugar and vanilla in large mixer bowl until creamy. Beat in egg. Gradually beat in flour mixture. Stir in oats, *¾ cup* morsels and *½ cup* walnuts. Spread into lightly greased 13 x 9-inch baking pan.

Measuring Oats

Measure oats as you would flour by spooning the oats into a dry measuring cup, then leveling them off with a straight-edged spatula. If you use the scoop-and-shake method, you will use more oats than you should, which will cause a dry cookie or bar.

Bake in preheated 350°F. oven for 22 to 28 minutes or until center is set. Immediately sprinkle with *remaining* morsels; let stand for 5 minutes or until morsels are shiny. Spread morsels; sprinkle with *remaining* nuts. Cool completely in pan on wire rack. Cut into bars. Makes 2½ dozen bars.

Chocolate Oatmeal Bars

Cream Cheese-Chocolate Chip Pastry Cookies

1 package (17¼ ounces) frozen puff pastry, thawed

1 package (8 ounces) cream cheese, softened

3 tablespoons granulated sugar

2 cups (11½-ounce package) NESTLÉ TOLL HOUSE Milk Chocolate Morsels, *divided*

Roll *1 sheet* puff pastry to 14 x 10-inch rectangle on floured surface. Combine cream cheese and granulated sugar in small bowl. Spread *half* of cream cheese mixture over puff pastry, leaving 1-inch border on 1 long side. Sprinkle with *1 cup* morsels. Roll up, starting at long side covered with cream cheese. Seal edge by dampening with water. Repeat with *remaining* ingredients. Chill for 1 hour. Cut rolls crosswise into 1-inch-thick slices. Place cut side up on parchment-paper-lined or lightly greased baking sheets.

Bake in preheated 375°F. oven for 20 to 25 minutes or until golden brown. Let stand for 2 minutes; remove to wire racks to cool completely. Makes about 2 dozen cookies.

Cream Cheese-Chocolate Chip Pastry Cookies (see recipe above)

nple Treats

Even when you're shy on time, you can still enjoy
home-baked cookies and bars, hot from the oven.
These bake-it-simple recipes use shortcuts and
baking mixes, making them ideal for busy
cooks and beginners. Choose from ten
decadent, spur-of-the-moment treats and
satisfy your sweet tooth the easy way.

Chewy Cocoa Brownies

1⅔ cups granulated sugar
¾ cup butter or margarine, melted
2 tablespoons water
2 eggs
2 teaspoons vanilla extract
1⅓ cups all-purpose flour

¾ cup NESTLÉ TOLL HOUSE Baking Cocoa
½ teaspoon baking powder
¼ teaspoon salt
¾ cup chopped nuts (optional)
   Sifted powdered sugar

Stir together granulated sugar, butter and water in large bowl. Stir in eggs and vanilla. Combine flour, cocoa, baking powder and salt in medium bowl; stir into sugar mixture. Stir in nuts. Spread into greased 13 x 9-inch baking pan.

Bake in preheated 350°F. oven for 18 to 25 minutes or until wooden pick inserted in center comes out slightly sticky. Cool completely in pan on wire rack. Sprinkle with powdered sugar. Cut into bars. Makes 2 dozen brownies.

Easy Butterscotch Chip Cookies

1 package (18½ ounces) chocolate cake mix
½ cup vegetable oil
2 eggs

1⅔ cups (11-ounce package) NESTLÉ TOLL HOUSE
   Butterscotch Flavored Morsels
½ cup chopped pecans (optional)

Combine chocolate cake mix, oil and eggs in large bowl. Stir in morsels and pecans. Drop by rounded tablespoon onto ungreased baking sheets.

Bake in preheated 350°F. oven for 8 to 10 minutes or until centers are just set. Let stand for 2 minutes; remove to wire racks to cool completely. Makes about 3½ dozen cookies.

Recipes pictured on page 78.

Super Easy Chocolate Mint Triangles

20 chocolate sandwich cookies, finely crushed
     (about 2 cups)
1½ cups chopped nuts
1½ cups (10-ounce package) NESTLÉ TOLL HOUSE
     Mint-Chocolate Morsels*

1 cup flaked coconut
1¼ cups (14-ounce can) CARNATION Sweetened
     Condensed Milk

Press crushed cookies onto bottom of greased 13 x 9-inch baking pan; sprinkle with nuts, morsels and coconut. Drizzle with sweetened condensed milk.

Measuring for Success

When baking, exact measurements are essential. Count on these basics for measuring success: Spoon flour, powdered sugar, granulated sugar or oats into a dry measuring cup and level off with a straight-edged spatula. Pack brown sugar into a dry measuring cup and level it off. Place morsels, nuts, raisins or coconut into a dry measuring cup to the top only, not overflowing. Pour liquids such as water, juice, syrup and oil into a liquid measuring cup, reading the measure at eye level.

Bake in preheated 350°F. oven for 20 to 25 minutes or until coconut is golden brown around edges. Cool completely in pan on wire rack. Cut into squares; cut each square in half diagonally to form a triangle. Makes 3½ dozen triangles.

*Note: NESTLÉ TOLL HOUSE Semi-Sweet Chocolate Morsels may be substituted for the mint morsels.

Pictured on page 78.

Chocolate Chip Cookie Brittle

1 cup (2 sticks) butter or margarine, softened

1 cup granulated sugar

1½ teaspoons vanilla extract

1 teaspoon salt

2 cups all-purpose flour

2 cups (12-ounce package) NESTLÉ TOLL HOUSE
Semi-Sweet Chocolate Morsels, *divided*

1 cup chopped nuts*

Beat butter, granulated sugar, vanilla and salt in large mixer bowl. Gradually beat in flour. Stir in *1½ cups* morsels and nuts. Press into ungreased 15 x 10-inch jelly-roll pan.

Bake in preheated 375°F. oven for 20 to 25 minutes or until golden brown and set. Cool in pan until just slightly warm.

Microwave *remaining* morsels in heavy-duty plastic bag on HIGH (100%) power for 1 minute; knead bag to mix. Microwave at additional 10-second intervals, kneading until smooth. Cut a small hole in corner of bag; squeeze to drizzle over cookie brittle. Allow chocolate to cool and set; break into irregular pieces. Makes about 2¼ pounds.

*Note: Omitting nuts could cause the brittle to become dry.

Clockwise from top right: Super Easy Chocolate Mint Triangles (see recipe, page 77), Easy Butterscotch Chip Cookies (see recipe, page 76), Chewy Cocoa Brownies (see recipe, page 76), and Chocolate Chip Cookie Brittle (see recipe above)

Rocky Road Squares

1 package (21½ ounces) fudge brownie mix calling for ½ cup water
Vegetable oil, per package directions
Egg(s), per package directions
½ cup CARNATION Evaporated Milk

2 cups miniature marshmallows
1½ cups coarsely chopped DIAMOND Walnuts
1 cup (6 ounces) NESTLÉ TOLL HOUSE Semi-Sweet Chocolate Morsels

Prepare brownie mix according to package directions, using oil and egg(s), except substitute evaporated milk for water. Spread into greased 13 x 9-inch baking pan.

Bake according to package directions; do not overbake. Remove from oven. Top with marshmallows, walnuts and morsels.

Bake for 3 to 5 minutes or just until topping is warmed and beginning to melt. Cool in pan on wire rack for 20 to 30 minutes. Cut into squares. Makes 2 dozen squares.

Top to bottom: Rocky Road Squares (see recipe above), Mini Morsel Shortbread Squares (see recipe, page 82), and Peanut Butter Chocolate Layer Bars (see recipe, page 83)

Mini Morsel Shortbread Squares

1 cup (2 sticks) butter or margarine, softened
¾ cup granulated sugar
1 egg
1 teaspoon vanilla extract

2¼ cups all-purpose flour
2 cups (12-ounce package) NESTLÉ TOLL HOUSE
Semi-Sweet Chocolate Mini Morsels, *divided*

Beat butter and granulated sugar in large mixer bowl until creamy. Beat in egg and vanilla. Gradually beat in flour. Stir in *1 cup* morsels. Press into bottom of ungreased 13 x 9-inch baking pan.

Bake in preheated 350°F. oven for 30 to 33 minutes or just until top begins to brown. Immediately sprinkle with *remaining* morsels. Let stand for 5 minutes or until morsels are shiny; spread. Cool completely in pan on wire rack. Cut into squares. Makes 4 dozen squares.

Pictured on page 81.

Peanut Butter Chocolate Layer Bars

20 peanut butter sandwich cookies, finely crushed (about 2 cups)

3 tablespoons butter or margarine, melted

1¼ cups lightly salted dry-roasted peanuts, chopped

1 cup (6 ounces) NESTLÉ TOLL HOUSE Semi-Sweet Chocolate Morsels

1 cup flaked coconut

1¼ cups (14-ounce can) CARNATION Sweetened Condensed Milk

Combine cookie crumbs and butter in small bowl; press into bottom of greased 13 x 9-inch baking pan. Layer peanuts, morsels and coconut over crumb mixture. Drizzle sweetened condensed milk evenly over top.

Bake in preheated 350°F. oven for 20 to 25 minutes or until coconut is golden brown. Cool completely in pan on wire rack. Cut into bars. Makes 2 dozen bars.

Pictured on page 81.

Triple Chocolate Cookies

1¾ cups all-purpose flour

½ cup NESTLÉ TOLL HOUSE Baking Cocoa

1 teaspoon baking soda

2 cups (12-ounce package) NESTLÉ TOLL HOUSE Semi-Sweet Chocolate Morsels, *divided*

⅓ cup butter or margarine, cut into pieces

1¼ cups (14-ounce can) CARNATION Sweetened Condensed Milk

1 egg

1 teaspoon vanilla extract

½ cup chopped nuts

Combine flour, cocoa and baking soda in medium bowl. Melt *1 cup* morsels and butter in large, *heavy* saucepan over *lowest possible* heat, stirring until smooth. Remove from heat. Stir in sweetened condensed milk, egg and vanilla; mix well. Stir in flour mixture. Stir in nuts and *remaining* morsels (dough will be soft). Drop dough by rounded tablespoon onto lightly greased baking sheets.

Bake in preheated 350°F. oven for 8 to 10 minutes or until edges are set but centers are still slightly soft. Let stand for 2 minutes; remove to wire racks to cool completely. Makes about 3½ dozen cookies.

Triple Chocolate Cookies (see recipe above) and Chocolate Fudge Brownies (Peanut Butter Brownie Variation) (see recipe opposite page)

Chocolate Fudge Brownies

1⅔ cups granulated sugar

½ cup (1 stick) butter or margarine

2 tablespoons water

2 bars (2 ounces *each*) NESTLÉ TOLL HOUSE
   Unsweetened Baking Chocolate, broken into pieces

2 eggs

1½ teaspoons vanilla extract

1⅓ cups all-purpose flour

¼ teaspoon baking soda

¼ teaspoon salt

½ cup chopped nuts (optional)

Microwave granulated sugar, butter and water in large, microwave-safe bowl on HIGH (100%) power for 4 to 5 minutes or until mixture bubbles, stirring once. (Or, heat granulated sugar, butter and water in medium saucepan just to boiling, stirring constantly. Remove from heat.) Add baking bars, stirring until melted.

Stir in eggs, one at a time, beating well after each addition. Stir in vanilla. Gradually stir in flour, baking soda and salt. Stir in nuts. Pour into greased 13 x 9-inch baking pan.

Bake in preheated 350°F. oven for 15 to 20 minutes or until wooden pick inserted in center comes out slightly sticky. Cool completely in pan on wire rack. Cut into bars. Makes 2 dozen brownies.

Peanut Butter Brownie Variation: Prepare batter as *above* without nuts; *do not pour into pan.* Combine ½ cup creamy or chunky peanut butter, 3 tablespoons granulated sugar and 2 tablespoons milk in medium, microwave-safe bowl. Microwave on HIGH (100%) power for 45 seconds; stir until smooth. Pour batter into pan. Spoon peanut butter mixture over top; swirl with spoon. Bake in preheated 350°F. oven for 20 to 25 minutes. Cool completely in pan on wire rack. Cut into bars. Makes 2 dozen brownies.

Lighte

Double Chocolate Chip Brownies sound more like an indulgence than a light snack, but take our word for it! These chocolate fantasy squares, along with all of the recipes in the Lighter Delights chapter, offer less than you bargained for—less fat and fewer calories—but all of the luscious taste you desire.

Delights

Sensibly Delicious Chocolate Chip Cookies (see recipe, page 88),
Slimmer Chocolate Crinkle-Top Cookies (see recipe, page 89) and
Double Chocolate Chip Brownies (see recipe, page 90)

Sensibly Delicious Chocolate Chip Cookies

3 cups all-purpose flour
1½ teaspoons baking soda
1 teaspoon salt
1¼ cups packed dark brown sugar
½ cup granulated sugar
½ cup (1 stick) margarine, softened

1 teaspoon vanilla extract
2 egg whites
⅓ cup water
2 cups (12-ounce package) NESTLÉ TOLL HOUSE Semi-Sweet Chocolate Morsels
⅓ cup chopped nuts (optional)

Combine flour, baking soda and salt in medium bowl. Beat together brown sugar, granulated sugar, margarine and vanilla in large mixer bowl. Beat in egg whites. Gradually beat in flour mixture alternately with water. Stir in morsels and nuts. Drop by rounded tablespoon onto lightly greased baking sheets.

Bake in preheated 350°F. oven for 10 to 12 minutes or until centers are set. Let stand for 2 minutes; remove to wire racks to cool completely. Makes about 5 dozen cookies. About 94 calories and 4 grams fat per cookie with nuts.

Pictured on pages 86 and 87.

Slimmer Chocolate Crinkle-Top Cookies

2 cups (12-ounce package) NESTLÉ TOLL HOUSE
   Semi-Sweet Chocolate Morsels, *divided*

1½ cups all-purpose flour

1½ teaspoons baking powder

¼ teaspoon salt

1 cup granulated sugar

2 tablespoons margarine, softened

1½ teaspoons vanilla extract

2 egg whites

¼ cup water

½ cup powdered sugar

Melt *1 cup* morsels in small, *heavy* saucepan over *lowest possible* heat. When morsels begin to melt, remove from heat; stir. Return to heat for a few seconds at a time, stirring until smooth. Cool to room temperature.

Combine flour, baking powder and salt in small bowl. Beat together granulated sugar, margarine and vanilla in large mixer bowl. Beat in melted chocolate; beat in egg whites. Gradually beat in flour mixture alternately with water. Stir in *remaining* morsels. Cover; chill until firm.

Shape dough into 1½ -inch balls; roll in powdered sugar to coat generously. Place on greased baking sheets.

Bake in preheated 350°F. oven for 10 to 15 minutes or until sides are set but centers are still slightly soft. Cool for 2 minutes; remove to wire racks to cool completely. Makes about 3 dozen cookies. About 100 calories and 4 grams fat per cookie.

Pictured on pages 86 and 87.

Baking Light Pointers

When baking light, be sure to follow the recipe directions carefully. Lower-fat cookies are less forgiving of mistakes than regular cookies, because they have less of the fat that provides structure, lends tenderness and moisture, and promotes browning. When margarine is specified, use regular stick margarine, not a "spread" or "diet margarine." Do not overbake. If you choose a dark baking sheet or pan, reduce the oven temperature by 25°F. For melt-in-your-mouth flavor, serve the cookies warm or microwave them for a few seconds just before serving.

Double Chocolate Chip Brownies

2 cups (12-ounce package) NESTLÉ TOLL HOUSE Semi-Sweet Chocolate Morsels, *divided*

1 cup granulated sugar

½ cup unsweetened applesauce

2 tablespoons margarine

3 egg whites

1¼ cups all-purpose flour

¼ teaspoon baking soda

¼ teaspoon salt

1 teaspoon vanilla extract

¼ cup chopped nuts (optional)

Heat *1 cup* morsels, granulated sugar, applesauce and margarine in large, *heavy* saucepan over low heat; stir until smooth. Remove from heat. Cool slightly. Stir in egg whites. Combine flour, baking soda and salt. Stir into chocolate mixture. Stir in vanilla. Stir in *remaining* morsels and nuts. Spread into greased 13 x 9-inch baking pan. Bake in preheated 350°F. oven 16 to 20 minutes or just until set. Cool in pan on wire rack. Cut into bars. Makes 2 dozen. About 159 calories and 7 grams fat per brownie with nuts.

Pictured on pages 86 and 87.

Lower-Fat Blonde Brownies

2¼ cups all-purpose flour

2½ teaspoons baking powder

½ teaspoon salt

1¾ cups packed brown sugar

6 tablespoons (¾ stick) margarine, softened

3 egg whites

1½ teaspoons vanilla extract

⅓ cup water

2 cups (12-ounce package) NESTLÉ TOLL HOUSE Semi-Sweet Chocolate Morsels

Combine flour, baking powder and salt in small bowl. Beat brown sugar, margarine, egg whites and vanilla in large mixer bowl until smooth. Gradually beat in flour mixture alternately with water. Stir in morsels. Spread into greased 15 x 10-inch jelly-roll pan. Bake in preheated 350°F. oven 20 to 25 minutes or until top is golden brown. Cool in pan on wire rack. Cut into squares; cut each in half diagonally to form triangles. Makes 3 dozen brownies. About 140 calories and 5 grams fat per brownie.

Good-for-You Choc-Oat-Chip Cookies

1¾ cups all-purpose flour
1 teaspoon baking soda
½ teaspoon salt
½ teaspoon ground cinnamon
1¼ cups packed dark brown sugar
½ cup granulated sugar
½ cup (1 stick) margarine

½ cup unsweetened applesauce
2 egg whites
1 tablespoon vanilla extract
2½ cups quick or old-fashioned oats
2 cups (12-ounce package) NESTLÉ TOLL HOUSE
Semi-Sweet Chocolate Morsels
½ cup chopped nuts

Combine flour, baking soda, salt and cinnamon in small bowl. Beat together brown sugar, granulated sugar, margarine and applesauce in large mixer bowl. Beat in egg whites and vanilla. Gradually beat in flour mixture. Stir in oats, morsels and nuts.
Drop by rounded tablespoon onto greased baking sheets.

Bake in preheated 375°F. oven for 9 to 10 minutes for a chewy cookie or 12 to 13 minutes for a crispy cookie. Let stand for 2 minutes; remove to wire racks to cool completely. Makes about 4 dozen cookies. About 120 calories and 5 grams fat per cookie.

Lower-Fat Blonde Brownies (see recipe opposite page) and Good-for-You Choc-Oat-Chip Cookies (see recipe above)

Marbled Chocolate Brownies

1⅓ cups all-purpose flour
⅓ cup NESTLÉ TOLL HOUSE Baking Cocoa
¼ teaspoon baking soda
¼ teaspoon salt
1¼ cups granulated sugar
1 cup (6 ounces) NESTLÉ TOLL HOUSE Semi-Sweet Chocolate Morsels

½ cup unsweetened applesauce
2 tablespoons margarine
3 egg whites
1 teaspoon vanilla extract
4 ounces light cream cheese (Neufchâtel), softened
1 tablespoon granulated sugar
1 tablespoon nonfat milk

Combine flour, cocoa, baking soda and salt in small bowl. Heat 1¼ cups granulated sugar, morsels, applesauce and margarine in a large, *heavy* saucepan over low heat, stirring constantly just until morsels are melted. Remove from heat. Cool slightly. Stir in egg whites. Add flour mixture and vanilla; stir well. Spread into a greased 13 x 9-inch baking pan.

Stir together cream cheese, 1 tablespoon granulated sugar and milk in small bowl. Drop by rounded teaspoon over batter; swirl over surface of batter with back of spoon.

Bake in preheated 325°F. oven for 22 to 28 minutes or just until set. Cool completely in pan on wire rack. Cut into bars. Makes 2¼ dozen brownies. About 110 calories and 3 grams fat per brownie.

Marbled Chocolate Brownie

Index

METRIC COOKING HINTS

By making a few conversions, cooks in Australia, Canada, and the United Kingdom can use these recipes with confidence. The charts on this page provide a guide for converting measurements from the U.S. customary system, which is used throughout this book, to the imperial and metric systems. There also is a conversion table for oven temperatures to accommodate the differences in oven calibrations.

Product Differences: Most of the ingredients called for in the recipes in this book are available in English-speaking countries. However, some are known by different names. Here are some common American ingredients and their possible counterparts:
- Sugar is granulated or castor sugar.
- Powdered sugar is icing sugar.
- All-purpose flour is plain household flour or white flour. When self-rising flour is used in place of all-purpose flour in a recipe that calls for leavening, omit the leavening agent (baking soda or baking powder) and salt.
- Light corn syrup is golden syrup.
- Cornstarch is cornflour.
- Baking soda is bicarbonate of soda.
- Vanilla is vanilla essence.
- Green, red, or yellow sweet peppers are capsicums.
- Golden raisins are sultanas.

Volume and Weight: Americans traditionally use cup measures for liquid and solid ingredients. The chart, below, shows the approximate imperial and metric equivalents. If you are accustomed to weighing solid ingredients, the following approximate equivalents will be helpful.
- 1 cup butter, castor sugar, or rice = 8 ounces = about 250 grams
- 1 cup flour = 4 ounces = about 125 grams
- 1 cup icing sugar = 5 ounces = about 150 grams
  Spoon measures are used for smaller amounts of ingredients. Although the size of the tablespoon varies slightly in different countries, for practical purposes and for recipes in this book, a straight substitution is all that's necessary.
  Measurements made using cups or spoons always should be level unless stated otherwise.

EQUIVALENTS: U.S. = AUSTRALIA/U.K.

⅛ teaspoon = 0.5 ml
¼ teaspoon = 1 ml
½ teaspoon = 2 ml
1 teaspoon = 5 ml
1 tablespoon = 1 tablespoon
¼ cup = 2 tablespoons = 2 fluid ounces = 60 ml
¼ cup = ¼ cup = 3 fluid ounces = 90 ml
½ cup = ¼ cup = 4 fluid ounces = 120 ml
⅔ cup = ½ cup = 5 fluid ounces = 150 ml
¾ cup = ⅔ cup = 6 fluid ounces = 180 ml
1 cup = ¾ cup = 8 fluid ounces = 240 ml
1¼ cups = 1 cup
2 cups = 1 pint
1 quart = 1 liter
½ inch =1.27 cm
1 inch = 2.54 cm

BAKING PAN SIZES

American	Metric
8×1½-inch round baking pan	20×4-cm cake tin
9×1½-inch round baking pan	23×3.5-cm cake tin
11×7×1½-inch baking pan	28×18×4-cm baking tin
13×9×2-inch baking pan	30×20×3-cm baking tin
2-quart rectangular baking dish	30×20×3-cm baking tin
15×10×1-inch baking pan	30×25×2-cm baking tin (Swiss roll tin)
9-inch pie plate	22×4- or 23×4-cm pie plate
7- or 8-inch springform pan	18- or 20-cm springform or loose-bottom cake tin
9×5×3-inch loaf pan	23×13×7-cm or 2-pound narrow loaf tin or pâté tin
1½-quart casserole	1.5-liter casserole
2-quart casserole	2-liter casserole

OVEN TEMPERATURE EQUIVALENTS

Fahrenheit Setting	Celsius Setting*	Gas Setting
300°F	150°C	Gas Mark 2 (slow)
325°F	160°C	Gas Mark 3 (moderately slow)
350°F	180°C	Gas Mark 4 (moderate)
375°F	190°C	Gas Mark 5 (moderately hot)
400°F	200°C	Gas Mark 6 (hot)
425°F	220°C	Gas Mark 7
450°F	230°C	Gas Mark 8 (very hot)
Broil		Grill

*Electric and gas ovens may be calibrated using Celsius. However, for an electric oven, increase the Celsius setting 10 to 20 degrees when cooking above 160°C. For convection or forced-air ovens (gas or electric), lower the temperature setting 10°C when cooking at all heat levels.